WEST SUSSEX WATERWAYS

P.A.L. VINE

First published November 1985
Reprinted November 1993

ISBN 0 906520 24 X

© P.A.L. Vine, 1985

Phototypeset by CitySet Ltd, Chichester

Published by Middleton Press
               Easebourne Lane
               Midhurst
               West Sussex
               GU29 9AZ
               Tel: (0730) 813169
(From 16 April 1995 - (01730) 813169)

Printed & bound by Biddles Ltd,
               Guildford and Kings Lynn

CONTENTS

ACKNOWLEDGEMENTS

I am very grateful indeed to the following people who have kindly assisted me or have lent me photographs: Fred Aldsworth, Michael Cardew, Mrs. Jenni Clarke, Bob Dawes, Roger Dunbar, Dendy Easton, Lord Egremont, Dr. Paul Girton, Richard Goodsell, Edward Griffith, Gerald Griffith, Tom Hendrick (Hon. Curator the Arundel Museum), Littlehampton Museum, Hayward Madden, Klaus Marx (Bluebell Railway Archives), Anthony Pagett, Fred Saigeman, Roger Sellman, Shoreham Port Authority, Stanley Smith, H.J.F. Thompson, Miss Edwina Vine, John Wood (Hon. Secretary of the Wey & Arun Canal Trust).

HISTORICAL BACKGROUND

Sussex established a reputation in the seventeenth century of having the most abominable roads in the kingdom. Contemporary accounts were rarely encouraging for trade or for the traveller. Daniel Defoe (1724) revealed that the roads were so impassable that even with teams of oxen hauling huge tree trunks, it could take two or three years to move timber from the Weald to the shipyards. Arthur Young (1768) enumerated the few miles of good road and of the rest wrote that 'it is a prostitution of language to call them turnpikes'. The county was therefore dependent on its waterways for moving heavy goods like timber and chalk between the country and the coast.

The rivers of West Sussex have a particular charm as they flow through green meadows and wide valleys before piercing the chalk ridge of the South Downs and pouring into the English Channel. Initially they were made navigable in the sixteenth century by straightening the worst sinuosities. A glance at a map showing the parish boundaries, which often followed the natural course of the rivers, will show where this has occurred. The stretch of the Arun below Pulborough Bridge is a good example. Further improvements were made in the late eighteenth and early nineteenth century by building artificial cuts with locks or canals. In 1790 the Arun Navigation Company even built a 375 yard tunnel to shorten the distance between Houghton and the upper reaches of the river by 3 miles.

The Arun Navigation in particular played the leading role in the county's transport system, indeed its history reflects on a smaller scale the evolution and decline of water transport in England. It began with the improvement of the river for navigation in the sixteenth century and continued until the arrival of the ubiquitous motor lorry in the nineteen twenties.

The ports – the meeting place of barge and coaster – were a scene of great activity. Arundel, Shoreham and Lewes were accessible to sea going craft of 300 tons and more. Colliers regularly transhipped coal for distribution inland to feed gas works, brickyards and the needs of householders. Attempts to develop a network of waterways between London and Sussex failed and it took many years before the sole water link between the Thames and the English Channel via the Wey & Arun Junction Canal could be effected in 1816. Seven years later the opening of the Portsmouth & Arundel Canal provided inland water communication between the naval dockyards of Portsmouth and Chatham. It was however a total failure due to the ending of the war with France and the fact that the route to London was circuitous and involved low bridges, shallows, narrows and the passage of 52 locks.

Insignificant perhaps in size and importance to the waterways of the Midlands and the North of England they nevertheless formed an integral part of the county's transport system for some three hundred years. Their financial success was limited but the benefits they brought to agriculture in particular and to the community in general were multifarious.

The waterways were at their busiest during the eighteen thirties when toll receipts of both the Arun Navigation and the Wey & Arun Junction Canal exceeded £2000 per annum. In 1839 the Arun Navigation Company freighted 36000 tons of cargo and paid a dividend of 12% on its £100 shares. In the same year the Wey & Arun carried 23000 tons but only paid a dividend of 1% since its share capital was eleven times greater than that of the Arun.

The gradual spread of railways across West Sussex brought them into competition with the waterways. The opening of the line from Shoreham to Chichester in 1846 was followed by lines to Petworth (1859), West Grinstead (1861), Arundel (1863), Cranleigh (1865) and Midhurst (1866). The Chichester & Arundel section of the Portsmouth & Arundel Canal was the first to become derelict in the 1850s whilst traffic on the remaining canals and navigation slowly dwindled in spite of stringent toll reductions on chalk and coal. By 1900 only the occasional barge was to be seen on the tideway of the rivers and on the Chichester Canal.

What is There to See Today?

The countryside explorer can discover the relics of a former age to remind him that these rivers and canals were once arteries of commerce. The hulk of some forgotten barge, the creeper-covered opening of a canal tunnel, a crumbling weir, the decaying chambers of old locks, the may-thorn clustered arches of stone bridges, the tiny dwellings proclaiming the former homes of wharfinger and lock-keeper.

The ravages of time have dealt less harshly with the abandoned lock-houses and embankments than have the local and water authorities who have in the guise of hygiene demolished many of the former and of flood protection bulldozed the latter. Their zeal to remove all traces of derelict buildings or to reduce the size of an area formerly liable to floods has resulted in what many regard as a waste of ratepayers' money and the destruction of our national heritage.

SUMMARY OF FACTS

Waterway	Terminal Points	Distance (miles)	No. Locks	Date Opened	Commercial Traffic Ceased	Whether Navigable (1985)
River Adur	Bines Bridge Mock Bridge Shoreham	14	3	1810*	1929	Yes – tidal
River Arun	Houghton Littlehampton	13½	none	c1550	1930	Yes – tidal
Arun Navigation	Newbridge Houghton	13	4	1790	1888	Canal sections Not navigable
River Arun	Pallingham Houghton	11½	none	c1560	1930	Yes – tidal
Baybridge Canal	West Grinstead Bines Bridge	3⅜	2	1826	1875	Canoes only. No public right of navigation
Chichester Ship Canal	Chichester Salterns	4	2	1822	1906	As far as Casher Lock, Birdham. Skiffs can be hired in Southgate Basin
Petworth Canal	Haslingbourne Bridge Shopham	1¼	2	1793	c1800	No
Portsmouth & Arundel Canal (barge section)	Ford Hunston	9	2	1823	1847	No
Rother Navigation	Midhurst Stopham	11½	8	1794	1888	Canoes only. No public right of navigation
Southwick Ship Canal	Portslade Southwick	1¾	1	1855	Open	Yes
Wey & Arun Junction Canal	Shalford Newbridge	18½	23	1816	1871	No. Short sections for canoes only

*The tideway was navigable from about 1600 but locks were not built until after the 1807 Act was passed.

1. George O'Brien Wyndham, third Earl of Egremont (1751–1837). He invested over £100,000 in developing inland navigation in West Sussex. As a result he was the sole owner of the Rother Navigation and the largest shareholder in the Arun Navigation Company, the Portsmouth & Arundel Navigation Canal Company and the Wey & Arun Junction Canal Company.

BAYBRIDGE CANAL

This must have ranked as one of the least known and least significant waterways in Britain. It was less than 3½ miles long and was contained entirely within the parish of West Grinstead. Although called 'a canal', it was really a river navigation with two lock cuts. In spite of its small size however the Act passed in 1825 ran to eighty printed pages.

The locality which the canal was to serve produced wheat of the finest quality and excellent timber, especially oak, and it was to enable these commodities to be sent more expeditiously to market that eight local landowners had petitioned for the Adur Navigation to be extended. Two of the petitioners, Lord Selsey and Sir Charles Burrell of Knepp Castle were well aware of the benefits of water carriage since the former was involved in the management of the Portsmouth & Arundel Canal and the latter through his close association with Lord Egremont (whose eldest daughter, Frances, he had married in 1808) and through being a shareholder and a member of the Wey & Arun Junction Canal Company Committee of Management for many years.

The Baybridge Canal Company was empowered to raise £9,000. £6,000 in fifty pound shares from amongst themselves and £3,000 by mortgaging the tolls. Mr. May Upton who had worked on the Wey & Arun Junction Canal (1814–6) had carried out the survey. He estimated that £5,958 would be required to make a navigation 28 ft wide, 4 ft deep with 2 locks 75 ft x 12 ft x 6 in, each having a 7 ft rise and also to rebuild Bines Bridge to allow barge traffic to pass.

Arthur Mant, the Storrington solicitor, was appointed clerk of the company. Tenders for excavating the canal were required by 16th September 1825 and the navigation was probably completed by the end of 1826. The main traffic was the import of manure and chalk and the export of wheat and timber. A wharf, limekiln and coal pens were built at the terminal basin at West Grinstead which adjoined the turnpike road to Horsham, five miles to the north. By 1830 Edmund Cartwright was writing in the county history that the canal 'has added to the advantages of communications; the increasing traffic of which proves its utility.'

The navigation was seldom used after the opening of the railway from Shoreham to West Grinstead in 1861. The preamble to the abandonment Act of 1875 makes reference to the traffic having of late years greatly diminished and the receipts being so reduced as to be insufficient to maintain the canal and yield a profit to the shareholders. The canal was closed on 1st September 1875.

One of the three petitioners for the Abandonment Act was Sir Percy Burrell, grandson of the third Earl of Egremont. The clerk was another generation of the Mant family. The company's responsibility for the maintenance of bridges and fences after the closure was met by paying compensation to the landowners from the monies received from the sale of land. The company also had to put 'in good and substantial repair public bridges, roads and culverts'.

The countryside explorer will find substantial remains of both locks, but no obvious sign of West Grinstead wharf.

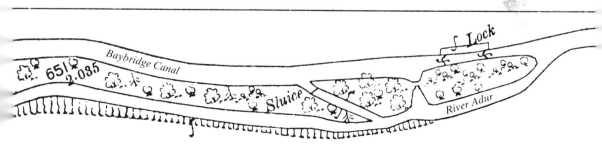

The first lock upstream in the Baybridge Canal was still shown on the 1896 25" scale map.

Baybridge Canal.

TO

Riverdiggers, Excavators,
BRICKLAYERS, AND OTHERS.

Notice is Hereby Given,

THAT THE

𝕭𝖆𝖞𝖇𝖗𝖎𝖉𝖌𝖊 𝕮𝖆𝖓𝖆𝖑 𝕮𝖔𝖒𝖕𝖆𝖓𝖞

WILL

Receive Tenders for excavating the Canal,

AND FOR

Building 2 Locks

THEREON, WITH

Bridges, Tumble Bays, and Sluices,

AS FOLLOWS, VIZ.,

For Casting Earth, at   per Yard cube.

Filling Earth, and wheeling not more than 20 Yards, at
   per Yard, cube.

Extra Stages of 25 Yards, at   per Stage.

Levelling, at   per Rood, of 64 Yards, superficial.

Puddling, at   per Yard, cube.

Building Locks, at   per Rod.

Building Bridges, Tumble Bays, & Sluises, at   per Rod.

Particulars may be known upon application to Mr. May Upton, at the Burrells' Arms Inn, at Westgrinsted, on or after Monday the 12th of September, Instant.

Tenders to be delivered at the Burrells' Arms Inn, before ten o'Clock in the Forenoon of the 16th of September, Instant, and the Persons making Tenders to attend the next Meeting of the Company at the Burrells' Arms Inn on that Day at Eleven o'Clock in the Forenoon.

ARTHUR MANT,

CLERK TO THE COMPANY.

Storrington, 8th September, 1825.

2. West Grinstead Lock in 1950 had well preserved walls and skeletal remains of its gates.

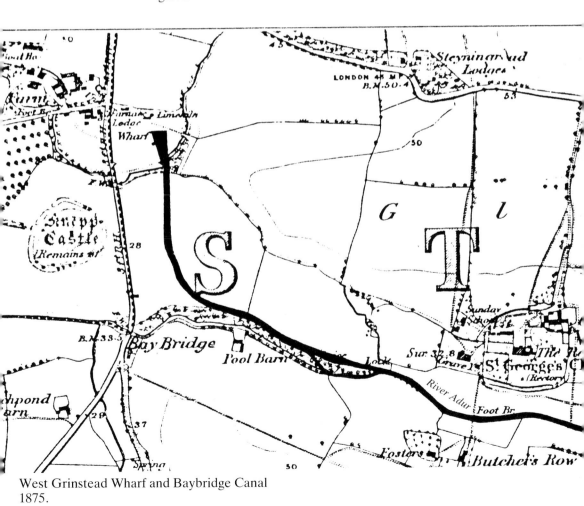

West Grinstead Wharf and Baybridge Canal 1875.

3. The lock near Lock Farm, Partridge Green, in 1952. The river Adur flows through the lock chamber whose walls remain in remarkably good condition.

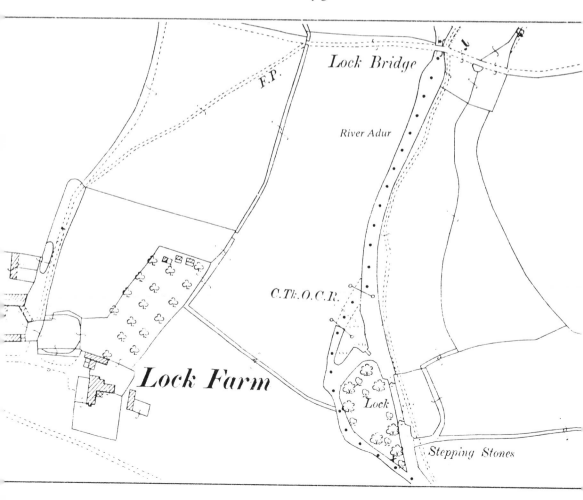

BAYBRIDGE CANAL,

IN THE PARISHES OF

WEST GRINSTEAD AND ASHURST,

SUSSEX.

NOTICE IS HEREBY GIVEN

That in pursuance of an Act of Parliament, which received the Royal Assent on the 14th day of June, 1875, being "An Act to provide for the Closing of the Baybridge Canal, and the Sale of the Site thereof,"

THE ABOVE

CANAL

WILL BE

CLOSED FOR TRAFFIC

FROM AND AFTER THE

1st Day of SEPTEMBER, 1875,

And all Rights of Way, or User, and other Rights in reference thereto, or in connection therewith, will become extinguished on and after such day, subject to the provisions of the said Act.

GEO. FRENCH MANT,

Clerk to the Company of Proprietors of the Baybridge Canal.

Storrington,
26th July, 1875.

W. W. MITCHELL, Printer, *West Sussex Gazette* Office, Arundel.

ADUR NAVIGATION

The River Adur was used for moving timber down to Shoreham Harbour in the eighteenth century but it was regarded by Joseph Priestly as a 'very imperfect tideway navigation' until it was improved between Shoreham and Bines Bridge with a branch to Mock Bridge by the Adur Navigation Act 1807. The cost of carrying out the work was met by an annual assessment of two shillings (10p) per acre on all lands lying in the level above Beeding Bridge during the years 1807–9. Seventy nine local landowners and freeholders together with the commissioners of sewers for the Rape of Bramber were appointed to execute the work. As the Adur was tidal to Bines Bridge it was not intended to make cuts or build locks but two locks were built, Bines Lock above the point where the Adur divides a mile below Bines Bridge, and one 150 yards above the bridge; the latter was probably constructed after the Baybridge Canal (q.v.) had been opened in 1826. Betley Lock was built a similar distance up the branch towards Mock Bridge Wharf. This wharf lay just downstream of the bridge at Shermanbury which was crossed by the Henfield to Cowfold turnpike as well as by that from Horsham. The locality was well wooded and bore good corn crops. What is not certain is whether barges could pass beneath Mock Bridge and reach Shermanbury Flour Mill.

The navigation was little used after the opening of the railway from Shoreham to West Grinstead in 1861. Betley lock was out of repair in September 1862 and was probably not reinstated. Traffic however revived between 1903 and 1929 when the Portland Cement Company used the river to barge clay from the pit at Horton to the Beeding Cement Works and cement to Shoreham Harbour. The average annual tonnage carried was about 17,000 tons with peaks of 22,000 tons in 1920 and 21,000 tons in 1925.

The estuary of the river Adur was like that of the Arun, subject to the constant drift of shingle which blocked its mouth from time to time and caused its mouth to move eastwards towards Brighton. New entances made in 1760, 1775, 1800 and 1810 silted up and it was not until 1821 that the present harbour mouth at Kingston could be finally established.

Toll receipts from the Navigation started well but fell away as the following table shows:–

1812	£523	1870	£20
1815	£475	1880	£7
1820	£329	1890	£4
1830	£174	1900	nil
1840	£270	1910	£121
1850	£126	1920	£279
1860	£119	1928	£243

4. A barge moored above Beeding Bridge in about 1905.

Mock Bridge Wharf 1875. Note the cut opposite the Wharf leading to Outlands Farm. The River Adur is marked with unequal dashes.

5. The Cement Works at Lower Beeding in about 1910. Barges brought clay from Horton to the Wharf and carried cement down to Shoreham Harbour for transhipment until March 1929. Note also the extensive railway sidings which linked up with the Horsham to Shoreham line.

6. The last train to cross the old wooden railway bridge over the Adur Navigation at Old Shoreham, on 8th June 1892. It was replaced by the present steel bridge, designed by Sir John Aird.

Towards the close of the 18th century the ferry at Old Shoreham became dangerous and was frequently impassible. Unlike Littlehampton which had to wait until 1907, Shoreham obtained the Act for its bridge in 1781. 500 feet long with 27 openings, its width was 12 feet with two recesses 70 ft x 24 ins for passing vehicles. It was opened in 1782 and taken over by the LB & SCR in 1862, who subsequently rebuilt it.

7. Shoreham Suspension Bridge in 1833 at high tide. Coastal shipping did not proceed up river as on the Arun or Ouse rivers so provision did not have to be made for an opening span. The bridge was designed by W. Tierney Clarke, the architect of Hammersmith and Marlow bridges. The bridge was demolished in 1922.

This unusual embellishment was on the title page of the Act of Parliament for building Old Shoreham Bridge in 1781.

8. An early nineteenth century view of shipping in the Western Arm of Shoreham Harbour at half tide. At high tide the river has the appearance of a lake but at low tide the stream trickles through a waste of mud.

9. Bungalow Town, on the south side of the mud flats bordering the Adur, was built from railway carriages beyond restoration. They were sold to property speculators who had them carted across the river. Sir Ralph Richardson (1902–1983) lived with his mother in two of these railway carriages when a boy. 'The carriages were joined by a tin roof. The space between the carriages made a large room. There was a front porch and verandah and a kitchen added at the back. So, we had a front door and a back door as well as about twenty side doors, these with brass handles and leather strapped windows. We had lamps and candles for illumination and we caught the rain water off the tin roof into a butt, and we boiled it for drinking.' Bungalow Town was occupied by the defence forces in 1940 and redeveloped after the war. Today only a few bungalows survive.

SOUTHWICK SHIP CANAL

This is formed by the old eastern arm of the river Adur which until 1760 (when the harbour mouth was at Aldrington) formed its main channel. The Shoreham Harbour Act 1760 enabled a new entrance to be cut at Kingston but the inexorable eastward drift of the shingle caused a further entrance to be made in 1821 at the site of the present entrance. The silted eastern arm was dredged to a depth of 15 feet and the entrance lock opened on 20th February 1855 to form a 1¾ mile canal to Aldrington Basin. The lock (175 ft x 31 ft) was replaced in 1933 by the Prince George lock (240 ft x 40 ft). The old lock was then converted into a dry dock. An additional lock, the Prince Philip (374 ft x 57 ft) was constructed adjacent to the Prince George lock in 1966 which can admit vessels of over 4,500 tons.

In the middle of the nineteenth century it sometimes happened that as many as 20 colliers would enter the harbour in one day. These far famed Shoreham sailing vessels traded regularly to Hartlepool for coal, to Honfleur, Caen and Le Havre for fruit, eggs and vegetables and to the Baltic and America for timber. The construction of the Brighton & Hove Gas Works in 1870 and the electricity generating station in 1897 resulted in great quantities of coal being imported. The extensive buildings of the gas company were demolished in 1973 and the 30 acre area redeveloped with wine and container terminals, a grain silo and a new turning bay.

10. The entrance locks to the Southwick Ship Canal. Nearest is Prince Philip Lock, opened in 1966, which is the largest in Sussex; the Prince George Lock was opened in 1933 to replace the original lock opened in 1855 which is now used as a dry dock. In this photograph the upper gates of the dry dock are visible with a vessel under repair in the lock itself.

The 1930 six inch scale map showing the entrance to Shoreham Harbour. The entrance lock to the Southwick Ship Canal is at the right.

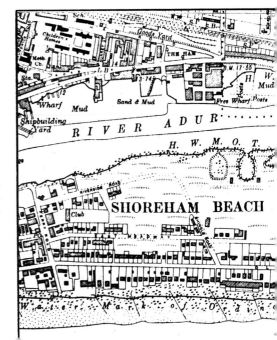

11. The Southwick Ship Canal at Portslade in 1908, looking east, with colliers discharging at the gas works.

1873 survey showing the gun platforms guarding the Brighton & Hove Gas Works, the timber pond and the steam cranes. Aldrington Basin (not marked) was then known as Wish Wharf.

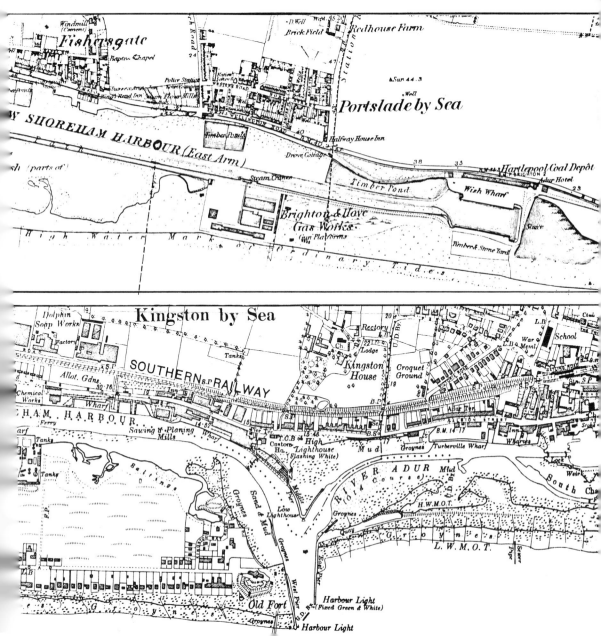

12. Midhurst Wharf, in about 1912, after Port's boat house had been burnt down.

Note the proximity of the gas holder to the canal basin.

ROTHER NAVIGATION

This was built by the third Earl of Egremont to enable coal to be imported to Petworth and Midhurst and to allow corn and timber to be exported. The line surveyed by William Jessop was completed in 1794 at a cost of £13,300. It followed the natural course of the river, rose 54 ft by eight locks, and had less than 2 miles of artificial cuts along its length of 11¼ miles. The navigation was a success. The purchase of land and the opening of the chalk pit at Amberley by Lord Egremont at the beginning of the nineteenth century led to some 4,000 tons of chalk being carried up the navigation to be burnt at the lime kilns adjoining the farms. While fertilization improved the quality of the crops, the reduced cost and facility of freighting coal increased grain production, since it proportionately lessened the demand for furze which had had to be grown to provide fuel for the kilns.

The completion of the railway to Midhurst in 1866 was the principal reason for the decline of the navigation although it remained in commercial use until March 1888.

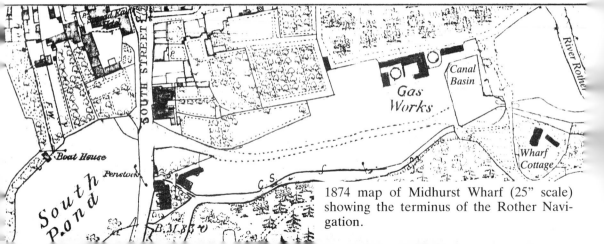

1874 map of Midhurst Wharf (25" scale) showing the terminus of the Rother Navigation.

13. Midhurst Wharf Cottage around 1900. The tow-path went beneath the bridge which was built in 1794 and is still in use. After the navigation ceased to be used for barge traffic in 1888, pleasure skiffs were kept in the basin.

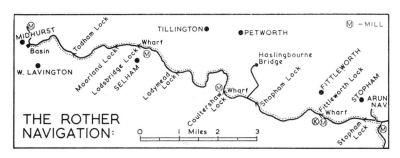

THE ROTHER NAVIGATION:

14. The entrance to Midhurst Canal Basin in 1962. The bridge was restored in 1977 as part of the town's commemoration of Queen Elizabeth's Silver Jubilee.

15. Moorland Lock in 1982.

16. Lodsbridge Lock in 1975, in process of being converted into a covered swimming pool.

←

17. Ladymead Lock which was the fifth lock above the Arun.

18. Selham Bridge around 1900.

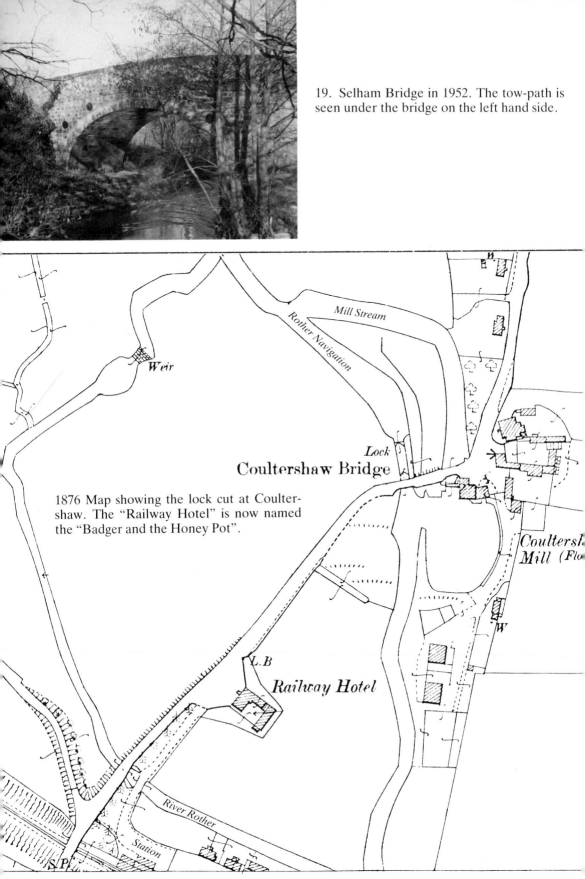

19. Selham Bridge in 1952. The tow-path is seen under the bridge on the left hand side.

Mill Stream

Rother Navigation

Weir

Lock

Coultershaw Bridge

1876 Map showing the lock cut at Coultershaw. The "Railway Hotel" is now named the "Badger and the Honey Pot".

Coultersh. Mill (Flo

L.B

W

Railway Hotel

River Rother

Station

S.P.

20. Coultershaw Flour Mill circa 1905. The mill was burnt down in 1923, later rebuilt in ferro-concrete and subsequently demolished.

21. Pleasure skiffs passing through the remains of Shopham Lock in 1895.

22. Shopham Lock Chamber in 1960. A weir has been built to replace the upper lock gates over which a boat can shoot when there is plenty of water.

23. Fittleworth Lock in 1899. The lower gates are clearly out of order.

24. Fittleworth Mill was best known because it was painted by John Constable. It ceased to grind corn towards the close of the nineteenth century.

25. A barge moored below Fittleworth Bridge, 1875.

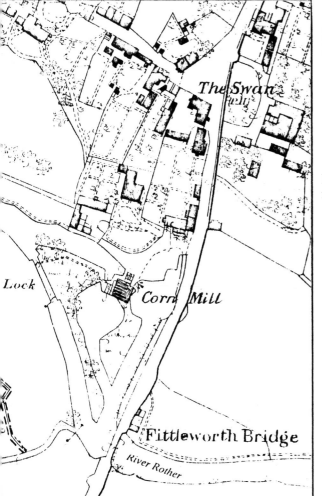

Fittleworth Bridge, Mill and Lock – 1876 map.

26. The canal bridge above Stopham Lock, built by William Jessop in 1792, looking east (1971).

27. The bridge on the lane between Stopham and South Barn Farm, circa 1900. It was just above Stopham Lock.

ABOVE THE LOCK.

28. Stopham Lock in 1960.

29. The entrance to the Rother Navigation, below Stopham Bridge in 1952. Currently the entrance channel is silted up and blocked by weeds.

PETWORTH CANAL

This was really no more than a canalized stream with two locks from the Rother Navigation at Shopham to Haslingbourne Bridge, a distance of 1¼ miles. Authorized by Parliament in the Rother Navigation Act of 1791, the Earl of Egremont had it in mind to extend the waterway to the Wey Navigation at Shalford. William Jessop considered that such a link was practicable. However opposition from landowners and a lack of enthusiasm by the proprietors of the Wey Navigation caused this idea to be dropped. There is however some evidence that the stream above Haslingbourne Bridge was improved but it was not used for navigation.

The canal appears to have carried little traffic after 1800 when a deviation was authorized by Parliament to allow the turnpike road from Chichester to pass by Coultershaw Mill instead of by Rotherbridge. The navigation is shown on the first edition of the one inch ordnance survey published in 1813 but the first edition of the six inch survey of 1875 shows that part of it had then been filled in and the locks removed.

In 1791 the turnpike road from Chichester to Petworth crossed the Rother at Rotherbridge and continued towards Tillington. It was not until 1800 that the road was diverted by Coultershall Mill and Rotherbridge was pulled down.

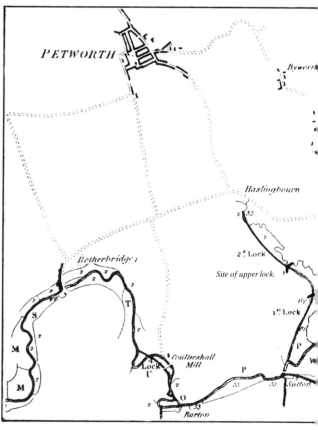

30. Haslingbourne Bridge in 1964. The bridge built in 1792 was widened in the 1970's but the original bridge remains. Barges formerly turned above the bridge.

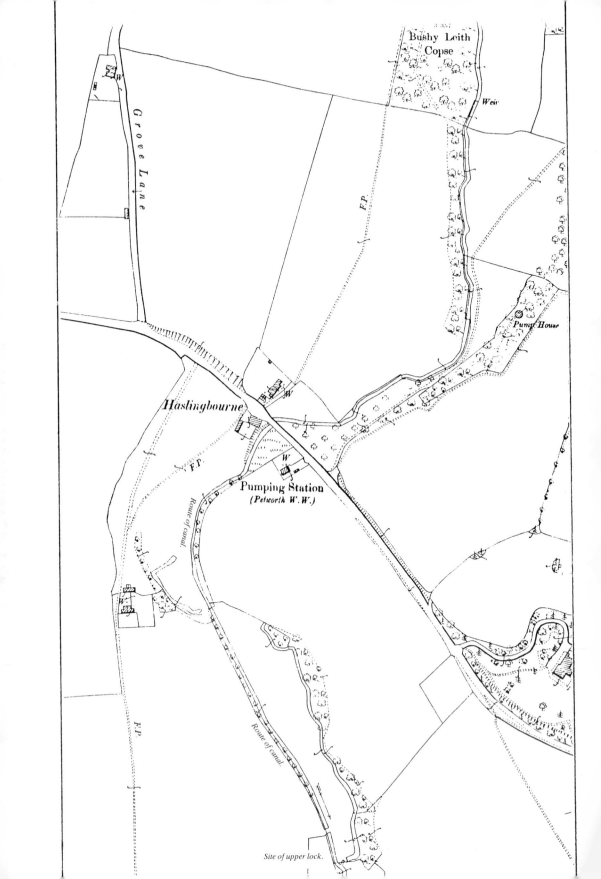

Bushy Leith
Copse

Weir

Grove Lane

F.P.

Pump House

Haslingbourne

F.P.

W

W

W

W

Pumping Station
(Petworth W.W.)

Route of canal.

F.P.

Route of canal.

Site of upper lock.

31. The bed of the Petworth Canal looking towards the Rother Navigation above Shopham Lock, visible after heavy rain in 1963.

Haslingbourne Bridge was the authorized terminal point of the Petworth Canal. The 1896 map still shows the bed of the old stream before its course was straightened in 1793.

PORTSMOUTH & ARUNDEL CANAL NAVIGATION

This linked Portsmouth to the Arun Navigation at Ford and was in four sections:
(i) The Portsea Ship Canal (2¼ miles) from the terminal basin of Halfway Houses to Milton capable of admitting 150 ton craft. 2 locks.
(ii) 13 miles of dredged channel from Milton across Langstone Harbour and round the north coast of Hayling and Thorney Islands to Birdham.
(iii) The Chichester Ship Canal (4 miles) from Birdham to Southgate Basin for 100 ton craft. 2 locks.
(iv) Barge canal from Hunston to Ford (9 miles). 2 locks.

A fifth section at Cosham was authorized but not made although in 1831 the tidal channel round Portsea Island was dredged to provide a direct link to Portsmouth Harbour.

The Navigation was completed in 1823 at a cost of £170,000 but now that the Napoleonic wars were over, trade suffered from competition with the coasting trade; furthermore the inland water route was circuitous and tedious. There were 52 locks between Portsmouth and London Bridge, tricky tidal channels, low bridges and often either too much or too little water. On Portsea Island salt water percolated from the canal into the wells, polluting water supplies.

In 1824, the Navigation's most successful year, traffic from London totalled 2,500 tons compared with 1,150 from Portsmouth. Barge masters being unable to obtain regular back carriage had either to return empty or under-laden. Corn and groceries were the main down cargoes with smaller shipments of items like eggs, soldiers' baggage and bullion for the Bank of England, back.

The Company never paid a dividend. The Portsea Canal was closed in 1827, the Ford-Hunston section ceased to be commercially used after 1847 and the Chichester canal in 1906.

The London–
Portsmouth
Barge Route:

DATES OF COMMERCIAL
USE INDICATED.

CANAL: ——————
RIVER NAVIGATION: ——————

0   5   10 MLS.

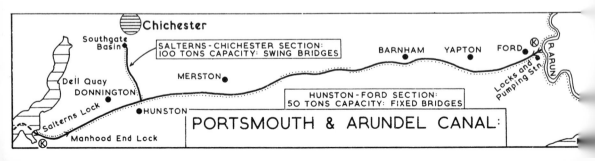

PORTSMOUTH & ARUNDEL CANAL:

32. The entrance to the Portsmouth & Arundel Canal at Ford, circa 1840. The upper (or second) lock is visible below the bridge which carried the road from Ford to Clymping. The pumping station housed a steam engine capable of lifting 96 hogsheads (5,000 gallons) of water a minute from the Arun. This rate was necessary as water could only be taken from the river for two hours after high water and one hour after low water, to prevent salt water entering the canal.

33. Ford Lock in about 1855. Traffic on the canal virtually ceased after the opening of the Shoreham to Chichester railway in 1846, in which year it was stated that it was used on average only once a week. It is said that the canal was last used in 1856 but the Chichester to London traffic ceased in 1840. The towpath bridge may have continued in existence until 1917 since the Minutes of the Commissioners of the Port of Arundel refer to its dilapidated state, at that time.

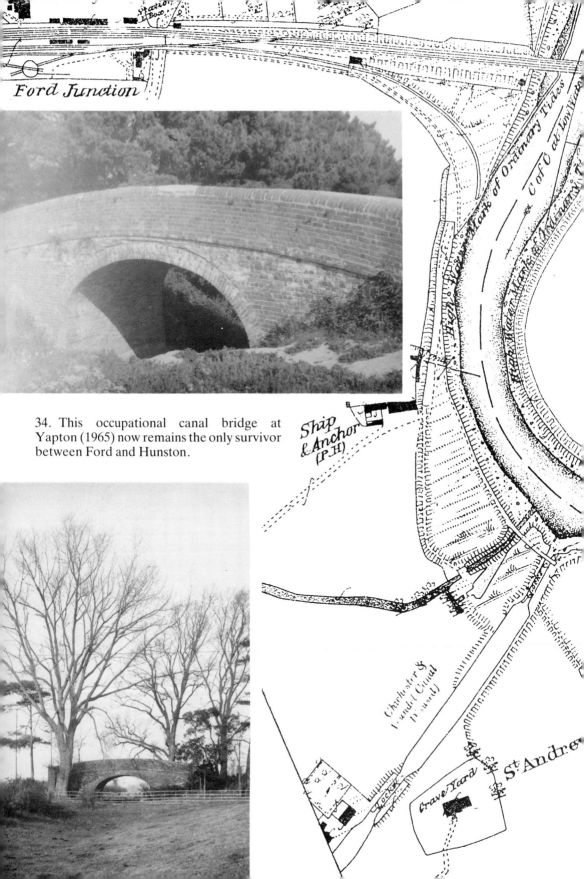

Ford Junction

34. This occupational canal bridge at Yapton (1965) now remains the only survivor between Ford and Hunston.

Ship & Anchor (P.H)

Chichester & Arundel Canal (Disused)

Grave Yard *St Andre*

The 1876 map showing the tow-path bridge and locks at the entrance to the Portsmouth & Arundel Canal at Ford, although the navigation had not been commercially used since 1847. A railway siding is shown, running onto a wharf on the River Arun.

36,37. Disused sections of the Portsmouth & Arundel Canal near Barnham and at North Mundham, 1952.

35. This occupational farm bridge over the dried up bed of the canal was photographed in 1964. The bridge has now collapsed and is almost entirely hidden by undergrowth.

THE CHICHESTER SHIP CANAL

This formed part of the Portsmouth & Arundel Canal Navigation which ran from Ford to Portsmouth.

The need to link Chichester with the sea stemmed from the fact that coastal vessels, particularly colliers, had to discharge their cargoes at Itchenor, for want of draught, into lighters which themselves had to be unloaded at Dell Quay, some 2 miles short of the city. Goods then had to be conveyed by wagon into Chichester, incidentally having to pass a turnpike gate on the way. In 1816, 18,000 tons of coal, besides 1,650 tons of merchandise, had been imported in this manner. The ship canal, 4 miles long with 2 locks, enabled barges receiving coals at Itchenor to proceed to the city direct. Six iron swivel bridges allowed vessels to berth in Southgate Basin. Opened in April 1822, the canal remained in commercial use until 1906. The waterway was formally closed in 1928 and sold to the West Sussex County Council in 1957. In 1984, the Chichester Canal Society leased part of the navigation and aims to maintain and restore the canal for recreational purposes.

Bradshaw stated in 1832 that craft up to 90 feet long, 18 feet 6 inches beam and with a draught of up to 5 feet 3 inches could use the waterway.

38. The Richmond Arms Inn on the west side of the canal basin. In 1845 Kelly's Directory of Sussex listed Clement Sayers, lime burner, the Richmond Inn. By 1855 Sayers had also become a coal merchant.

39. Southgate Basin, Chichester 1962. Although it has not been used commercially since 1906, the basin has recently been cleared out and is now leased by the West Sussex County Council to the Chichester Canal Society.

40. The gas holders in 1963. The gas works were opened in 1823 some eighteen months after Southgate Basin had come into use. The carrying of coal was the most important function of the canal throughout its history. Although collier brigs sometimes unloaded at the basin, the normal practice was for coal to be transhipped into barges in the channel of Chichester Harbour.

41. Circus elephants bathing in Southgate
Basin in 1903.

42. The approach to Southgate Basin in
about 1870.

43. Dudley Swing Bridge around 1890. The
iron swivel bridges which crossed the ship
canal between Southgate Basin and Chichester
Harbour were made in 1820 by Tickell of
Southampton. All were named after sup-
porters of the canal – hence Casher, Crosbie,
Cutfield, Dudley, Egremont and Poyntz.

44,45. Poyntz Swing Bridge at Hunston 1962. W.S. Poyntz (1770–1840) who had married the sister of the 8th Viscount Montague, lived at Cowdray House, and was MP for Chichester in 1826. The entrance to the barge canal to Ford and Arundel was filled in in 1896, but a hump remains in the road to Selsey to this day. The bridge has been removed for preservation and has been replaced by a fixed structure, with a generous headroom for pleasure boats.

46. This unusual drawbridge carried the Hundred of Manhood & Selsey Tramway over the Chichester Canal near Hunston. The line operated from 1897 to 1935. This picture was taken shortly after it had opened.

47. Saddle tank 0–6–0 *Sidlesham*, built in 1861, is seen crossing the canal in about 1920.

48.–50. Casher Lock, Birdham, in 1954. It was named after Edward Casher (who became Mayor of Portsmouth in 1843) and was situated just west of the main road to the Witterings.

51. Salterns Lock at the entrance to the Chichester Canal (1952). After being derelict for many years, the lock was reopened for pleasure craft in 1932 and remains usable today.

WEY & ARUN JUNCTION CANAL

The Wey & Arun Junction Canal linked the Wey Navigation at Shalford with the Arun Canal at Newbridge near Wisborough Green thus providing an inland water route from the Thames at Weybridge to the English Channel at Littlehampton. Although an attempt to link the rivers Wey and Arun had been made in 1641 the Parliamentary bill failed to pass through the House of Lords (see London's Lost Route to the Sea chapter III) and it was not until 1813 that an Act of Parliament was obtained. The canal was surveyed by Josias Jessop, a son of William Jessop and constructed first by Zachariel Keppel, a local contractor of Alfold who went bankrupt and then completed by May Upton, the Petworth surveyor.

The canal was opened for traffic on 29 September 1816. Its total length was 18½ miles and the main engineering works consisted of 18 locks, over 30 bridges and two small aqueducts at Bramley and Drungewick. Besides serving the villages of Bramley, Wonersh, Cranleigh, Alfold, Dunsfold and Loxwood, it formed the only inland water link between the Thames and the English Channel.

The cost of building the canal was £107,000; £99,550 was raised by the issue of 905 shares of £100 at £110 each and the balance by mortgaging the tolls. The largest shareholder was George O'Brien Wyndham, the 3rd Earl of Egremont who held 250 shares or 28 per cent of the equity. The highest dividend paid on the £100 shares was 1%; the last of 6/- per cent was distributed in May 1866.

Barges from the coast brought seaweed for the farms, grain for the watermills, coal for the gasworks and a wide variety of groceries and merchandise for the village stores; they returned loaded with bark, farm produce, flour, forest timber and items like hoops and the other products of rural industry. Local traffic consisted mainly of chalk, clay, sand and gravel from the pits to the kilns and wharves at villages and farms. Exceptionally, the waterway from Portsmouth to London saw barges guarded by red coats carrying bullion to the Bank of England; more frequent were the cargoes of eggs, wine, old rope, rags and soldiers' baggage. Occasionally their manifest showed oddities like acorns, bullock horns, burr stones, carrots, cyder and fruit.

The tonnage carried was never substantial. It averaged only 9,000 tons until the opening of the Portsmouth & Arundel Canal in 1823 when it rose to an average of 16,000 tons during the next seven years.

In spite of the virtual demise of the London to Portsmouth trade the average exceeded 18,500 tons during the 1830's. Although the peak tonnage of 23,250 in 1839–40 was never surpassed, it did not drop below 10,000 tons until after the opening of the Guildford-Horsham Railway in 1865. An Act of Abandonment was obtained after much difficulty in 1868 which allowed the canal to be officially closed on 22 July 1871.

Barges however continued to trade to Bramley Wharf until 27 June 1872. The land and buildings belonging to the canal company were gradually sold back to the riparian owners.

Although many writers and countryside explorers have bewailed the loss of this waterway over the past eighty years, serious efforts to reopen the canal only began in 1970 with the formation of The Wey & Arun Canal Society, later to become the Wey & Arun Canal Trust. It now has 700 members and has successfully raised money through sponsored walks, jumble sales and from donations. The Trust has been responsible for clearing and dredging five miles of the canal bed, putting Rowner and Mallam locks back into working order and rebuilding numerous bridges and culverts. The Shalford Natural History Society cleared and repaired Tanyard Bridge at Gosden in 1977. Similarly the Pulborough Society was among those who contributed to the cost of rebuilding Pallingham Quay Bridge which was re-opened in 1976. Before the line of the former waterway can be restored however, formidable difficulties remain to be overcome since some landowners who now own some 13 miles of the canal bed do not wish a public right of way to divide their land. The fact that a large housing estate has been built upon the canal bed at Bramley will also necessitate a new line of waterway being cut. The prospects for the navigation being fully restored

are therefore uncertain. Much will depend on the results of a cost feasibility study currently being undertaken, the attitude of the Surrey and West Sussex County Councils, the Southern Water Authority, the forty or so riparian landowners and the continued enthusiasm of the many voluntary workers who have already been toiling amidst the undergrowth and mire for more than a decade.

52. Until the Wey & Arun Canal Trust began restoring locks in the nineteen seventies, most of the brick built locks had been plundered for their bricks. This picture shows Southland Lock near Ifold being demolished in about 1930.

53. Baldwins Knob Lock in 1952.

54. The Onslow Arms at Loxwood ("three beds or so" in 1857) bordered the Wey & Arun Canal and was frequented by bargees en route to Arundel or Guildford and the Thames. The road bridge over the canal would have appeared between the bank at the left hand corner of the inn and the bungalow at left.

55. The ruins of Drungewick Aqueduct in
August 1952. The autumn floods that year
washed away the remaining arches.

56. The site of Drungewick Aqueduct near
Loxwood in 1955.

57. The Northward approach to the entrance to Drungewick Lock 1953. The lock chamber, built of blocks of Pulborough stone in 1815, is now criss-crossed by fallen trees.

58. The bridge over the canal at Hope Farm was in imminent danger of collapse in 1952.

59. Brewhurst Lock Loxwood in 1952.
Although the canal had been disused since
1871 the lock gates remained standing until
the late 1970's.

60. Upper gates of Baldwin's Knob Lock in 1952. All the lock chambers of those below Southlands were built of blocks of Pulborough stone.

The Canal entered West Sussex in Gennets Wood, a rural location about 1½ miles north of Loxwood.The water level of the canal was 100 feet above the Liverpool datum at the county boundary and 8 locks were needed for the canal to descend 63½ feet to the Arun Navigation at Newbridge.

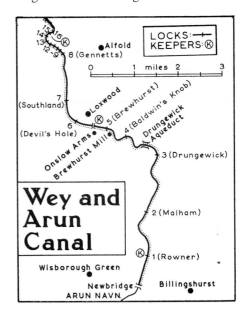

61. Rowner Lock as seen in about 1910. The
last barge had passed through from London
in 1871.

62. Rowner Lock in 1843. The cottage, where Charles Baverstock lived and worked for more than fifty years, was demolished in the nineteen thirties.

63. Rowner Lock after restoration by the Wey & Arun Canal Trust 1982. The first powered craft through!

64. Northlands Lifting Bridge, built by the Wey & Arun Canal Trust in operation in 1982.

TOLLS

PAYABLE ON THE WEY AND ARUN JUNCTION CANAL,
On and after the 1st June, 1855.

	s d	d	s d
COALS..............at 1 0 ℔ ton passing the whole line, or 1		per ton ℔ mile not to exceed 1 0 ℔ ton
TIMBER............at 2 0 ℔ ton ditto		or 2	per ton ℔ mile not to exceed 2 0 do.
GROCERY..........at 1 6 ℔ ton ditto		or 1½	per ton ℔ mile not to exceed 1 6 do.
BARK.............. at 1 6 ℔ ton ditto		or 1½	per ton ℔ mile not to exceed 1 6 do.
HOOPS & CORN....at 1 6 ℔ ton ditto		or 1½	per ton ℔ mile not to exceed 1 6 do.
SLATE & IRON ....at 1 6 ℔ ton ditto		or 1½	per ton ℔ mile not to exceed 1 6 do.
BRICKS & TILES ..at 1 0 ℔ ton ditto		or 1	per ton ℔ mile not to exceed 1 0 do.
CHALK & LIME'....at 1 6 ℔ ton ditto		or 1	per ton ℔ mile not to exceed 1 6 do.
FIRE WOOD .. ..at 1 6 ℔ ton ditto		or 1½	per ton ℔ mile not to exceed 1 6 do.
SEA GRAVEL AND SEA WEED at 1 3 ℔ ton ditto		or 1	per ton ℔ mile not to exceed 1 3 do.
DUNG (from London) at 1d. per ton per mile—not to exceed 1s. per ton for the whole line.			

LIGHT BARGES 1s. AT EACH END OF THE LINE OF CANAL.

65. Rowner Mill in 1957. It was unfortunately
burnt down in the 1960's.

←———————

66. The Canal Bridge carrying the A272 at
Newbridge in 1953. The tow-path passed
beneath on the right hand side.

ARUN CANAL

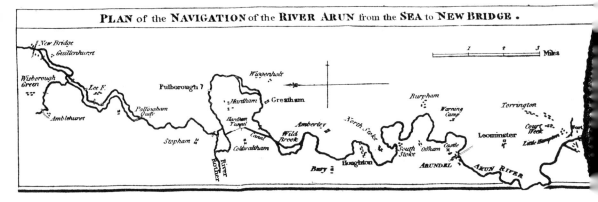

PLAN of the NAVIGATION of the RIVER ARUN from the SEA to NEW BRIDGE.

Probable date of this plan is 1791

Newbridge Wharf on the 1876 25" scale map, with the 6" scale map inset for location purposes.

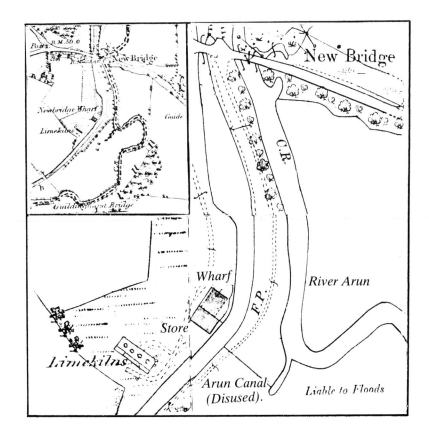

67. Newbridge Wharf, the terminus of the Arun Navigation. In August 1823 William Cobbett passed by 'Soon after quitting Billingshurst', he wrote, 'I crossed the river Arun, which has a canal running alongside of it. At this there are large timber and coal yards, and kilns for lime. This appears to be a grand receiving and distributing place.' Billinghurst and the surrounding farms and villages looked to the wharf at Newbridge for the arrival of their coal and groceries, for their fertilizers and fancy goods from London, Guildford and Arundel, and as the most convenient means of dispatching their own wares and farm produce to market. The warehouse was not built until 1839. Since the navigation was closed in 1888, the building has been used as a barn. Until the 1930's ledgers recording the barges' manifest were still kept there. It is hoped that one day it can be turned into a museum for the Wey & Arun Canal Trust.

The church spire shown on the company's seal is that of Wisborough Green, which was 1½ miles from the Arun Canal's terminus at Newbridge Wharf.

68. Orfold Aqueduct carried the canal over the river Arun. This photograph taken in 1955 shows that the west wall had fallen, revealing the brick floor of the aqueduct.

71. Middle Lock at Lee Farm (1952). The locks on the Arun Canal had single upper and double lower gates.

$\longrightarrow$

69,70. The remains of the flood gate below Orfold Lock in 1952. It was close to the river at this point which regularly damaged or washed away the canal embankment during the winter rains.

72. Toat Farm Bridge, recently restored by the Wey & Arun Canal Trust and the Pulborough Society.

←

74. Benjamin Stone was lock-keeper at Pallingham from 1871 to 1888. He continued to live in the keeper's cottage until shortly before his death in 1935. ⟶

75. John Stephney, who lived at Hay Barn on the Lea Place Estate in 1952 when he was 86, remembered working on the barges going up to Newbridge in the 1880's.

←

73. Pallingham Quay Bridge was restored in 1976.

←

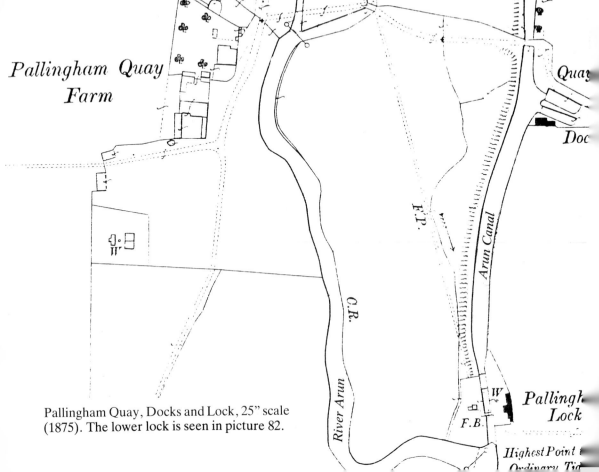

Pallingham Quay, Docks and Lock, 25" scale (1875). The lower lock is seen in picture 82.

76. The Carpenter's Shop (1886) built of timber and thatch where Benjamin Stone used to work. The docks were between the tree trunks and the two huts, in this southward view.

←

77. Entrance to Pallingham Docks and the barge building yard, in 1952. It is a brave man who attempts to penetrate the all embracing thicket which covers the area.

78. Pallingham Lock. This sluice is immediately above the upper gates. When the iron lock paddle was winched up, the water drained into the lock chamber from the canal pound to fill the lock. Note the brick lined floor of the lock chamber.

79. The entrance to Pallingham Lock in about 1918. The lock cottage when sold by the Stopham Estate in 1911 included a bakery and grocery shop. It was let to Ben Stone at £7-4s-0d p.a.

80. Pallingham Lock in 1934. ——————→

81. Pallingham Lock chamber in 1952.

The date when the brick works at Harwood Green opened is not known but it was probably early in the nineteenth century. This map shows them as they were in 1876. Their output was barged downstream to Pulborough and Arundel. They ceased to operate about 1905 and are shown in the 1909 survey as disused. The dashes indicate the River Arun.

82. Fully laden barges had insufficient water to enter Pallingham Lock and so a lower lock was constructed in 1822 which increased the depth of water over the cill of the upper lock by 18 inches. The lower gate posts can be seen in this 1934 photograph. ⟶

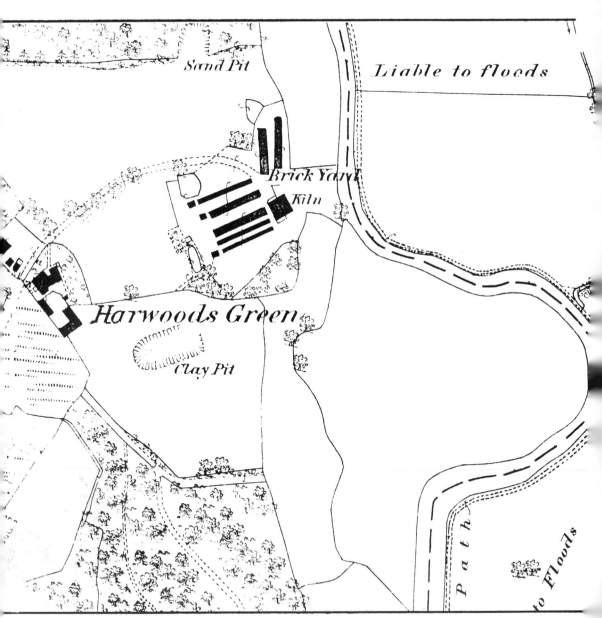

83. Before the WWI the reach above Stopham Bridge was the setting of the annual regatta. A similar regatta was held at Arundel. This picture was taken in 1912. ⟶

84. The *Reliance* of Fittleworth moored above Stopham Bridge, in 1905 with Bargemaster Sam Strudwick and Loyal Saigeman.

85. A closer view of Loyal Saigeman on the *Reliance* above Stopham Bridge, in 1905.

86. Stopham Wharf in about 1875. The central navigation arch is to the right and the bridge's remaining arches are hidden by trees. Even so the bridge's elevation appears distorted and there are in fact three not two arches to the left of the central arch. Artistic licence in the extreme.

←———

88. Stopham Bridge was built during the reign of Edward III. In the seventeenth century a drawbridge facilitated the passage of boats. In 1822 the central arch was raised to allow more heavily laden barges to pass. This oil painting by Henry King dates from before WWI.

←———

87. The boat-house at Stopham House around 1950. It was built soon after the turn of the century and was much used at the time of the local regatta. Only its foundations remained after the great flood of 1968 when the high wall beside the main road was also swept away.

COLDWALTHAM CUT

Part of the Arun Navigation on a 1791 plan, showing the distance saved by the Coldwaltham Cut and Hardham Tunnel compared with the river via Pulborough.

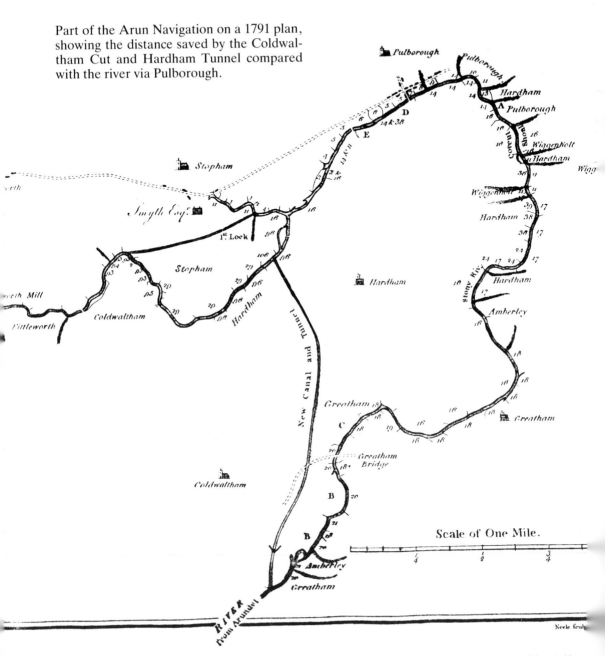

Scale of One Mile.

1876 map – scale 6" to the mile. Interesting points are:–

(i) There was no tow-path through Hardham Tunnel. Horses were led over the top but beneath the Pulborough-Petworth railway opened in 1859. A bridge carried the tow-path over the line to Arundel opened in 1863.

(ii) The tow-path went past Hardham Lock and along the Rother Navigation but did not reach Stopham Bridge.

(iii) There was no boat-house at Stopham House.

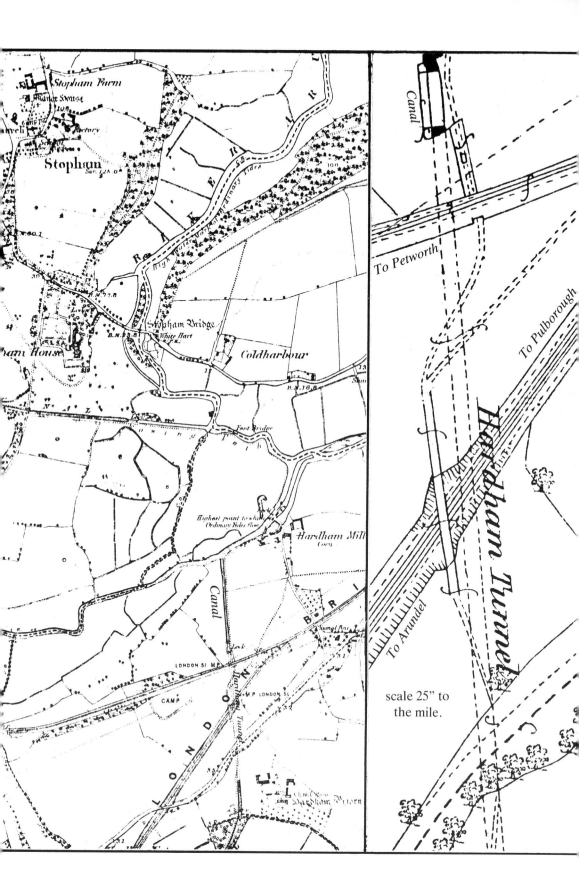

Stopham Farm

Manor House

Stopham

Stopham Bridge
White Hart

Coldharbour

ham House

Foot Bridge

Highest point to which
Ordinary Tides flow

Hardham Mill
Corn

Canal

CAMP

LONDON 51 M.

M.P LONDON 51.

Hardham Priory

Canal

To Petworth

To Pulborough

Hardham Tunnel

To Arundel

scale 25" to
the mile.

89. Hardham Mill, as it appeared in 1843. The lock cottage and gates can be seen on the right. The corn mill was bombed in 1941 and demolished It is now part of the site of the Southern Water Authority's pumping station.

91. The entrance to Hardham Lock in 1955. The Lock Keeper's cottage was demolished in 1957.

90. The north end of Hardham Tunnel, 1843. Observe the crude tree trunks used as beams for the lock gates.

92. The north entrance to Hardham Tunnel,
in 1951.

93. Upper gate of Hardham Tunnel Lock in 1951.

94. Hardham Tunnel – north entrance. The dam was built by the water authority on the site of Tunnel Lock in 1952. Note the state of preservation of one of the lock beams which had formed part of one of the gates. The tunnel was blocked beneath the railway lines in 1898. The entrance to the brick underpass for horses which was built when the Pulborough – Petworth railway was opened in 1859 was to the left above the tunnel.

95. Hardham Tunnel (1952). The floor of the 375 yard tunnel was also lined with bricks.

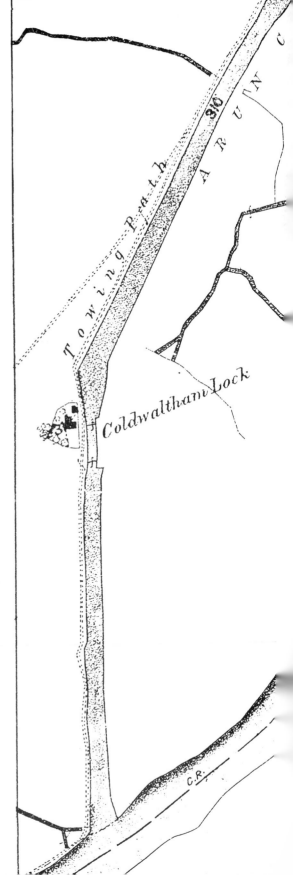

96. The south entrance to Hardham Tunnel in 1949. The hole is still visible (1985) but is now barred.

97. The entrance to Coldwaltham Lock at low tide in 1933. ⟶

98. Entrance to Coldwaltham Lock showing the ruined lock-house as it was in 1941.

ARUN NAVIGATION

The River Arun was made navigable to Stopham Bridge during the reign of Queen Elizabeth I. By 1637 barges could reach Pallingham Quay. The Arun Navigation Act, 1785 enabled the Arun Canal to be built to Newbridge and for the five miles of twisting river between Greatham and Pulborough to be avoided by means of the Coldwaltham cut which was carried beneath Hardham Hill and the London road by means of a 375 yard long tunnel. The cost of the canal and the tunnel was the substantial sum of £16,000.

The opening of the Wey & Arun and the Portsmouth & Arundel canals enabled improvements to be made to the navigation in the early 1820's. Consequently traffic increased from 17,600 tons in 1810 to 26,500 tons in 1824 and 36,000 tons in 1839.

The opening of the railways to Petworth (1859) and Arundel (1863) and the closure of the Wey & Arun Junction Canal in 1871 caused trade to drop from 20,000 tons in 1860 to 10,000 tons in 1870 and 5,000 tons in 1885. The Arun Canal was closed in 1888 but barge traffic continued to use the tideway until the late nineteen twenties, the Strudwicks of Fittleworth, the Doicks of Pulborough and the Henlys of Bury being the last barge-masters on the navigation.

99. Clements Bridge, Pulborough looking downstream, in 1843.

100. The same bridge in 1895, looking upstream. The low clearance, especially at times of flood, hindered barge traffic and was one of the main reasons for building the canal tunnel. The stone bridge fell into ruinous condition and was swept away in the flood of September 1968.

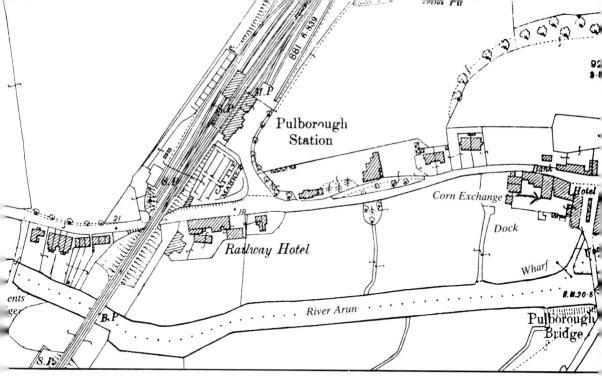

Pulborough in 1896.

101. Swan Bridge, Pulborough in 1891. Note the entrances to the dock which was also used as a wharf for unloading grain at the Corn Exchange.

Talberg bridge from S.S. Martins

102. Floods were always a handicap to navigation in the Arun Valley as can be seen from these pictures taken in the nineteen twenties of the London road at Pulborough.

◄————

104. A similar view taken in 1923. The wooden boat-house survived until 1940.

103. Swan Bridge, Pulborough, in 1843. The temple was built by Dr. Peter Patrick Martin, the Sussex archaeologist in 1793.

◄————

105. No. 64 below Pulborough Bridge in 1898 with Bargemaster Henry Doick and his sons Percy and Tom. In the space of seven years (1895–1901) he made 521 voyages up and down the Arun carrying 17,096 tons of cargo between Littlehampton and Pulborough. His average load was 33 tons, the maximum 38. The principal consignments were chalk, coal, culm, gravel and sand, but from time to time Doick carried ballast for Littlehampton brigs, steam coal for Arundel, bolts of reeds and osiers for Pepper & Son at Houghton, gas coal to Greatham and flints for the Duke of Norfolk at Timberley and for the Rector of Pulborough. Additional earnings arose from pile driving and usually once or twice a year no. 64 was hired out to Mr. Slaughter of York House School, Brighton, for barge parties to the 'Black Rabbit' and picnics in South Woods. Doick delivered a barge load of coal to Greatham Wharf on 19 April 1902. It was to be his last. Six months later he died at the age of 55.

106. Greatham Bridge was built in 18th century. The iron section was inserted in the early nineteenth century to allow barges more headroom.

107. Burpham Wharf by moonlight circa 1863, from a painting by W.H. Mason. The building of the Mid-Sussex Railway in 1861–2 involved cutting a new channel at Offham to avoid the need for two swing bridges across the navigation. Their cut shortened the distance between Arundel and Houghton but also resulted in barges no longer passing the wharf unless unloading there.

108. Bury Wharf in about 1910 showing one of Henly's barges under repair. Barges could only be refloated at high water spring tides. In 1925 the Southdown Bus Company commenced services from Horsham to Littlehampton via Bury and by 1930 the ubiquitous motor lorry had made barge work unprofitable. Henly sold his fleet of three barges and commercial use of the river above Arundel ceased. The skiff by the foot-bridge was the ferry boat which operated until 1957, taking pedestrians bound for Amberley across the river.

109. Houghton Wharf, looking south in about 1905. In the background are the quarries of Pepper & Sons limeworks which now are the site of the Chalk Pits Museum. Amongst a wide variety of industrial exhibits, there is a display of local canal relics.

1912 6" scale map of Houghton Wharves and Amberley Chalk Pits.

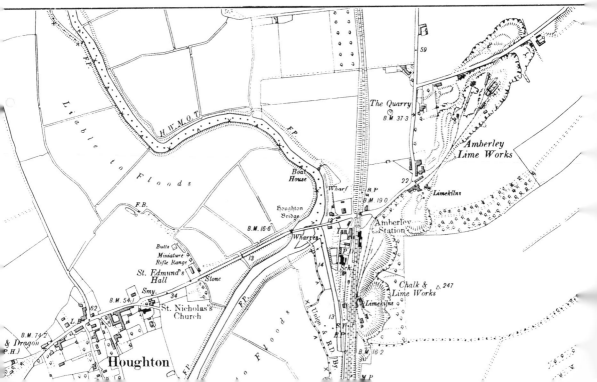

110. Houghton Bridge and an Amberley Chalk Pit in 1954.

111. No. 64 awash at Houghton Wharf in about 1910. Numbering was a relic of the Arun Navigation's system of licensing. On the Wey Navigation barges were known by their names. In 1830 those of the Arundel Barge Company were listed as *Arun, Commerce, Egremont, Norfolk, Sovereign, Swallow* and *Union*.

112. Lord Egremont built a cut 350 yards long from the river south of Houghton Bridge to enable barges to moor as close as possible to the chalk pits he had developed on land he had bought in 1800. In this illustration a barge is seen lying in the cut about 1905. Arthur Young writing in 1808 reported that Houghton pit was supplying some 40,000 tons of chalk annually, much of which was carried up the Arun to the kilns at Pulborough and Newbridge and to the Rother Navigation. Chalk continued to be carried from the Amberley Chalk Pits by water until 1914. ◄━━━━

114. The post-mill at Portreeves Acre above Arundel Castle circa 1850, after a painting by F.W. Watts. The mill was erected in 1769 and dismantled in the 1870's.

113. The *Swift* abandoned in Lord Egremont's Cut in 1934. The hulks of two barges were still visible here thirty years later.
◄━━━━

115,116. Here we see the different methods used to navigate the Arun in the 1820's. Until the tow-path was built (it reached Houghton in 1823) barges were either poled up or downstream with the tide or sailed. Later steam power was also used.

117. A steam tug was used between Little-hampton and Arundel from 1856 to 1914 and horse towage continued to be used until 1914 between Arundel and Amberley.

→

1875 25" scale map of Arundel.

118. Arundel Docks in about 1820. Note the entrance to the docks at bottom right.

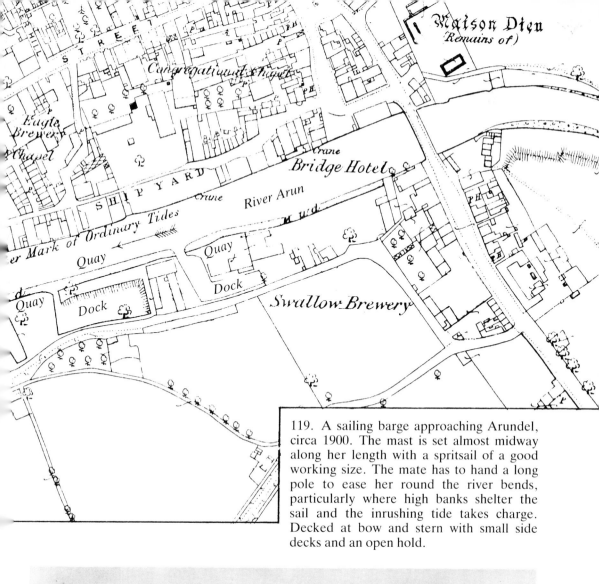

Maison Dieu
(Remains of)

Congregational Chapel

Eagle
Brewery

Chapel

Bridge Hotel

Crane

SHIPYARD

Crane

River Arun

Mud

Mark of Ordinary Tides

Quay

Quay

Dock

Quay

Dock

Dock

Swallow Brewery

119. A sailing barge approaching Arundel, circa 1900. The mast is set almost midway along her length with a spritsail of a good working size. The mate has to hand a long pole to ease her round the river bends, particularly where high banks shelter the sail and the inrushing tide takes charge. Decked at bow and stern with small side decks and an open hold.

121. One of the most characteristic views of Littlehampton for half a century. Because of the strong ebb and flow of the river, sailing vessels had difficulty both in entering the harbour unassisted and sailing between Littlehampton and Arundel. The Commissioners of the Port of Arundel had employed two pilots since 1793 and later experimented with various steam tugs. *The Newcastle* was in service from 1856 charging 3d a ton to tow a vessel in and out of the harbour, 4½d to Ford and 6d to Arundel and back. This was later reduced to 2d, 3½d and 5d. In 1889 the steam paddle tug *Jumna* was purchased for £1,400.

120. In spite of determined opposition from the Arun Navigation Proprietors, the London & Brighton Railway Company obtained its Act to build a line from Shoreham to Chichester which involved building a drawbridge across the Arun at Ford. The telescopic bridge had a sixty foot opening which took two men and a boy at least five minutes to open. Delays in opening the bridge to river traffic led to claims for compensation. £5 was the usual compensation paid for a 45 minute hold-up but in April 1858 a delay of 1 hour 50 minutes to the steam tug and her tow, the brigatine *Arun* resulted in £10 being paid. In 1862 the timber drawbridge was replaced by a double track lift and roll iron structure. Although this had a centre span of 90 feet, the width of the navigable passage was reduced to 40 feet. This bridge took half an hour or so to open as all the wires passing over had to be disconnected. Strengthened in 1898, it remained substantially unaltered until it was replaced by a fixed bridge in 1938 when the railway was electrified.

122. *Jumna* is seen towing a brigantine out of the harbour past the pier with its 'pepperpot' lighthouse built in 1848 (replaced 1948) and tower windmill built in 1831 and which continued working until 1913. The mill was demolished in 1932 when Butlin's Amusement Park was built. As sailing vessels came to be fitted with auxiliary engines, the need for tugs diminished and in 1914 *Jumna* was sold for £400.

Further Reading

A detailed account of the history of the navigations, which linked London to Arundel and Portsmouth, will be found in London's Lost Route to the Sea, P.A.L. Vine. A fully revised 4th edition is due to be published in March 1986 (David and Charles).